Old DRYMEN
and the BLANE and ENDRICK

by
John Hood

A floral display at Drymen Station. Stationmasters had good standing in their communities and this was reflected both in the way they and their staff conducted themselves, and in the way they maintained their stations. To encourage good service, companies like the LNER organised 'best-kept station' competitions. Floral displays were one element of these and since the communities also valued the accolade it was not unknown for floral contributions to be handed into the station by residents prior to the annual inspection.

© John Hood, 2000
First published in the United Kingdom, 2000,
by Stenlake Publishing, Ochiltree Sawmill, The Lade,
Ochiltree, Ayrshire, KA18 2NX
Telephone / Fax: 01290 423114

ISBN 1 84033 109 7

ACKNOWLEDGEMENTS

The publishers wish to thank Hugh and Jessie McArthur for permission
to reproduce the pictures in this book from their collection.

In 1860 the Blane Valley Railway Company announced their intention to construct a line through the Blane valley to provide a shorter and cheaper alternative to the existing Forth & Clyde Junction line (opened in 1857) which followed the course of the River Forth. This new line, officially opened on 1 July 1867, commenced at Lennoxtown and terminated at Dumgoyne. In 1882 the Strathendrick & Aberfoyle Railway Company further extended the line northwest to Gartness, on the Forth & Clyde Junction line. This extension dramatically affected the valley communities for not only was travel enhanced for the ordinary passenger, but goods could be transported more quickly and cheaply (speed being especially important to farmers transporting milk to urban areas). On occasion the Royal Train would also use the line whenever Edward VII was travelling to Duntreath Castle, home of his mistress, Mrs Alice Keppel.

INTRODUCTION

The villages featured in this book lie on or near the banks of both the River Endrick and the Blane Water. The latter rises in the Campsie Fells and drops steeply into the rich fertile valley of Strathblane, before joining the River Endrick and flowing into Loch Lomond. With the exception of Blanefield, which developed around the former Blanefield Calico Print Works, these villages originated as 'fermtouns' – for example, Drymen – or owed their existence to the railway, as in the case of Croftamie. Some, like Balmaha and Buchanan were originally little more than private fiefdoms of the landowning Buchanan family.

It was due to the richness of the soil that both the Blane and Endrick valleys were, from the earliest times, farming areas. Some of the villages also benefited throughout the eighteenth century from their proximity to the old drove roads. Drovers from the Highlands and Western Isles, heading for the cattle markets at Falkirk and Stirling, would regularly stay in the area in order to fatten their cattle on its lush pastures before going on to sell them in the markets. Monthly markets and fairs were held in some communities and even after the droving trade ceased these continued in villages such as Drymen.

Apart from Blanefield, the area had little industry. One exception was a small pyroligneous industry at Balmaha. Whisky was also distilled – both legally and illegally – in several places. However, the greatest number of factory workers were employed in the two printworks at Netherton, which were in operation throughout most of the 1800s. The presence of these factories encouraged people to settle in the immediate vicinity and, in turn, this created a need for housing which meant that new communities were formed, such as Blanefield.

The coming of the railway had a major impact on the villages and by 1867 there were two railways within the area, the Forth & Clyde Junction line and the line opened by the Blane Valley Railway. When these were eventually linked, life in the valleys was transformed.

Besides opening up the area to tourists, the railway provided local farmers with access to new markets for their produce and enabled villagers to travel further afield with greater ease. In common with places such as nearby Balfron and Killearn, this latter change particularly affected working patterns, for it became feasible for people to find employment in nearby towns, and today, even though the valleys continue to rely on farming, many locals still commute to workplaces outside the area.

In the late Victorian era schemes were instigated to give poorer children from the cities a holiday in the country. One of these was the Poor Children's Fresh Air Fortnight run by Glasgow Corporation's Education Department. Many large country houses were converted for use as homes for these schemes, one being the Marchioness of Montrose Home at Balmaha. It was opened in May 1891 and continued to serve this function until the outbreak of the Second World War, when it was commandeered by the Ministry of Defence to house munitions workers. For a brief period after the war it was used as a hotel and, when this venture failed, was converted to an outdoor centre. When this closed, the house lay derelict until it was converted into flats in 1994.

Balmaha, on the shores of Loch Lomond, originally comprised of little more than a factory and a pier, both owned by the Duke of Montrose. The factory was established in the 1800s to produce pyroligneous acid for use in the printworks of the Vale of Leven and Glasgow. In this picture the wood used in the production of the acid is seen piled up by the lochside at the pier. The wood principally came from the Duke's estate, where it was felled and cut before being stockpiled near the factory (which is to the left, just out of picture). Until 1896 the Duke's supply was supplemented with peeled branches discarded by the basket makers at Aberfoyle. At its peak the factory used 700 tons of wood annually. The factory closed in 1920 after which time the Duke sold the land. The house beside the wood stockpile (which was possibly the factory manager's home) is now Bay Cottage and above this, on higher ground, is the Marchioness of Montrose Home. The Duke's private yacht, *Violet*, is moored in Balmaha Bay.

BALMAHA LOCH LOMOND.

A.5775.

The Loch Lomond area has always been a popular destination and by 1817 the number of tourists visiting it was such that a steamship, the P.S. *Marion*, was built solely for cruising the loch. The Loch Lomond Steamship Company was formed in 1835 and by the 1850s there were three steamers operating on the loch in competition with one another. In time, a series of piers (similar to this one pictured at Balmaha) was built and a programme of regular sailings put into operation, thus enabling passengers to visit the many villages on the lochside and explore the surrounding countryside.

After the factory closed in 1920, Balmaha began to develop itself principally as a tourist destination. From this time on, many visitors were boating enthusiasts seeking to take advantage of the good anchorage provided by the sheltered Balmaha Bay. By the time of this 1937 view more properties had been built and Bay Cottage (hidden behind trees) had become a bed and breakfast establishment. Today, a small – but growing – marina has been established in the bay. Nearby is the recently established Loch Lomond Park Centre.

Balmaha

The name 'Balmaha' is said to derive from 'Mayhew' or 'Maha', a local saint. This view shows the Old Oak Tree, at one time a local landmark. The building beyond is the Balmaha Tea Room, built by the Duke of Montrose on the site of his factory. The tea room burnt down in 1971 and today the site is a landscaped picnic area. The building opposite is Bay Cottage and the white building on the extreme right is now the Highland Way Hotel.

War Memorial Museum, Buchanan

Buchanan, or to give it its full name, Milton of Buchanan, was originally the mill town of the Buchanans, one of the oldest families in the area. At one time they owned over 100,000 acres of land stretching from Loch Lomond eastwards towards Stirling. Their principal seat was at Buchanan Castle, near Drymen, and the head of the family ultimately carried the title Duke of Montrose. Many of the Dukes are buried in the graveyard at Buchanan Church. The War Memorial Museum at Buchanan was built in 1922 and, until 1937, housed a collection of local artefacts. Although now bereft of its turreted cones and castellated wall, it is otherwise unchanged and now functions as the village hall. The properties on the opposite side of the road include Burnside Cottage, which once housed the village school and schoolhouse prior to Buchanan Primary School and a new schoolhouse being built. The new school can be seen adjacent to the hall, with the schoolhouse lying further down the road.

Drymen's Main Street around the turn of the century. The substantial terraced housing on the left is certainly quite impressive in length, particularly given how many families it would house in relation to the population of Drymen at that time. Among the properties on the opposite side is the small single-storey Plough Inn, which dates from 1758. In the distance is Hawthorns which was built in 1820 on the site of thatched cottages.

MAIN STREET, DRYMEN.

A.7786

By the 1950s quite a few changes had taken place in the street. All the properties are still standing today although the terraced building (which continues to comprise of houses and shops) has been renovated, Hawthorns is a bed and breakfast establishment, and the property to the right of the picture is now the Poachers Rest restaurant.

Buchanan Arms, Drymen.

The Buchanan Arms Hotel in Main Street was originally a small country inn adjoining a farmhouse and was one of the first inns travellers would encounter on the old drove road from Balloch to Stirling. Until 1860 it was owned by the Buchanans of Drumnakill who sold it to the 4th Duke of Montrose, in whose family it remained until David Burnett bought it in 1935. He carried out an extensive modernisation programme, although only doing so after securing an agreement from the Electricity Board that Drymen (and therefore the hotel) would be supplied with electricity! During the 1980s the hotel was extended on several occasions and for a period was known as the Buchanan Highland Hotel. It is presently owned by Scottish Highland Hotels and now boasts a leisure centre and swimming pool. Pictured is the original two-storey building which still forms part of the hotel.

WAR MEMORIAL AND POST OFFICE, DRYMEN.

A.5752.

This 1937 view shows the village shop and post office at the corner of Gartness Road. This was built in 1820, at the same time as Hawthorns, and was originally a private dwelling called the New House. Further along is the Poachers Rest restaurant and, adjacent, the Salmon Leap Inn (formerly the Plough Inn). Barely visible to the right is the frontage of Primrose Bank. At one time this housed the shops of John Hutchison, the local baker, and latterly, Calum MacDonald, the butcher. Drymen's war memorial, on the corner beside Primrose Bank, was unveiled in 1921 by Field Marshall Earl Haig. Primrose Bank was demolished in 1974 when the new road to Balmaha was constructed and new housing erected on the site.

At the heart of Drymen is the Market Square – nowadays simply referred to as the Square – where in days gone by highlanders and lowlanders met to barter and hire. At the time of this 1899 view the long two-storey building that runs along the Square's western edge contained a mixture of living accommodation and business premises including a butcher, a joiner and the seventeenth century Drymen Inn. The latter, once owned by the Duke of Montrose, is now the privately-owned Winnock Hotel but retains much of the character of the original inn.

As it stood on a major drove road, it is not surprising that Drymen became a centre for the many livestock markets held throughout the year – at one time there was a weekly market and as many as eight fairs per year. In addition there were two main markets held every April and November. Village shows still take place annually, usually in June, on ground beside Drymen Bridge. Although this photograph dates from 1899, most of the properties shown here still remain. The small white thatched roof cottage on the extreme left is now the taxi office and next door but one is the Clachan Inn. The villa between them was built in 1864. In the middle of the picture is the Hawthorns and on the right is the post office and village shop.

The Clachan Inn, pictured on the left, was strategically situated in the Square at the junction of the roads leading north to Aberfoyle, east to Stirling and south to Glasgow. Built in 1734, the inn is said to be the oldest in Scotland and was at one time owned by Jean Gow, who was reputedly related to Rob Roy. It no longer has its thatched roof but it is still in business. Gilfillan's on the corner was a drapers and shoe merchant, stocking the once well-known 'Kiltie' brand of shoes. This shop is now The Great Outdoors.

THE SQUARE, DRYMEN.

212996.J.V.

By the 1930s the Clachan Inn had acquired a tiled roof and a reading room and library had been built just beyond Hillside and Braeside. In addition, the donkey and cart had been replaced by an Albion bus and a Morris car! The shop on the corner was still a drapery but had new owners, while the white-washed building next to this had become the Holly-Bush Tea Rooms. The police box at the corner of the Square is the one structure that has not survived.

Holly-Bush Tea Rooms, Drymen.

The Holly-Bush Tea Rooms were on Stirling Road, just off the Square. For a period they were run by a Mrs Robertson, whose engineer son built the Robertson engine (used to power the Cowal car) in his Drymen workshop in the 1920s. The Robertson engine can now be seen in Glasgow's Museum of Transport. When the tea rooms closed a Chinese take-away took over the premises. This closed in the mid-1990s and the Drymen Tandoori is now housed there. The building itself is largely unaltered, although a sloped roof extension has replaced the entrance way porch.

READING ROOM, DRYMEN.   308/27.

In 1829 a reference library containing approximately 400 titles was established in Drymen to serve the parish. Many of these early libraries were set-up by the local church or parochial board and, as such, the range of books would be quite limited: in Drymen's case the books were mainly about religion, history or travel. This reference library was replaced in 1910 by the Reading Room seen here. This held a wider range of books than its predecessor and it took newspapers. Nowadays, there is a new library on the Square but the Reading Room still plays a part in village life as a community hall.

This 1910 view is taken from Gartness Road, looking west towards the Square. It presents quite a rural picture but nowadays a modern bypass bisects Gartness Road. Just right of centre is the rear of Drymen United Free Church on Stirling Road. This was built in 1819 and later merged with the Parish Church. In the far distance, just left of centre, can be glimpsed the Winnock Hotel on the Square.

The Strathendrick Golf Course and Clubhouse, which was opened on 5 October 1901 by Lady Helen Graham, is situated on the outskirts of Drymen, on high ground overlooking the River Endrick. The clubhouse, pictured here shortly afterwards, is basically unchanged today, although a small extension has been added to the left. For many years members and friends of the club were entertained annually by the Duke of Montrose at nearby Buchanan Castle. The golfers pictured here are teeing off from the par 3 Whins.

DRYMEN STATION.

A.3568.

Drymen Station, 1936. When the *New Statistical Account* was published in 1839, Kilmaronock Parish (in which Drymen Station was situated) had no village. In fact, it was observed that 'there are not even four dwelling-houses in [the parish] closely contiguous'. This situation had little changed some eighteen years later when a railway station was opened about one-and-a-half miles south of Drymen, but some houses were soon built around the station and they became known as Drymen Station. When the station closed, the area was then absorbed into Croftamie. The long, low buildings in the distance (opposite the station) include Croftamie Cottage, a portion of which was a grocer's shop in the 1880s.

In 1853 proposals were unveiled by the Forth & Clyde Junction Railway Company to construct a railway line from Stirling, via Buchlyvie, to Balloch. Although it provided a service to farming communities along the Carse of Stirling, its primary purpose was to transport coal from mines in Fife to the industrial centres on Clydeside. Drymen Station, which was situated on this line, was opened on 26 May 1856. It was manned by a staff of six, with the stationmaster also acting as the village postmaster. As happened elsewhere, the railway suffered from competition from the bus companies and in 1934 passenger services were withdrawn. From then on the line was only used by goods trains, but in 1959 it closed completely. Although the station building is still in use as a private dwelling, the track has been lifted and the route now forms part of the West Highland Way.

POST OFFICE, DRYMEN STATION.

Edmond Terrace on the Glasgow to Drymen road, pictured here around 1925, was built to accommodate employees of Edmond's Sawmill. This had been established in the first half of the nineteenth century, but was destroyed by fire in 1937 and never replaced. While Edmond Terrace remains today, the old smiddy in the centre (converted into a garage in 1940 and owned in the 1980s by Drymen Motors) has been demolished. The site is occupied by the premises of KSM International Limited. To the extreme right is the post office which closed in 1964. This building has also been demolished and the post office relocated to the former Bungalow Rest Tea Room.

THE BUNGALOW REST, CROFTAMIE, DRYMEN STATION.

In the late 1940s Croftamie had two tea rooms, one of which was the Bungalow Rest which stood at the T-junction where the road to Pirnie Hall meets the Glasgow to Drymen road. The tea room closed in 1965 and the village post office moved in to the premises, where it remains to this day. Now named Burnbrae Cottage, the property itself is largely unchanged, although all but one of the chimneys have been removed and a garage has been added to one side.

PIRNIE HALL LODGE

The lodge in this 1914 photograph is one of two (East and West) which served Pirnie Hall, seen in the distance through the trees. The Hall was built in 1896 for the Murray family and remained in their hands until after the Second World War, when it and the two lodges were sold separately. Thereafter, the hall itself had several owners. It was ultimately acquired by Strathclyde Regional Council's Education Department for use as a residential conference/training centre for, amongst others, school pupils and young musicians. However, this function ceased in 1993 and the building is currently awaiting redevelopment. The East Lodge, shown here, has been a private residence since the Murray family sold it and, as such, has had several names, including White Gables. It is currently known as Witches Hat – no doubt because of its distinctively shaped roof.

New school and schoolhouse, Croftamie, Kilmaronock

The *New Statistical Account* of 1839 reported that there was one parochial and two unendowed schools within Kilmaronock Parish. By 1906, when this photograph was taken, a new school and schoolhouse had just been built at the edge of Croftamie on the main road to Drymen. The school was officially opened on 2 April 1907, at which time the Kilmaronock Public School was closed. Since many of the children had to walk a considerable distance to this new school, closures brought about by, say, inclement weather were always welcomed! The children were also sometimes given the day off for special occasions such as the launching of the R.M.S. *Queen Mary* in 1936, which many people flocked to see. The school was closed in the late 1990s and the pupils were transferred to the more modern Drymen Primary School. Since then Croftamie Nursery have used the building while the schoolhouse is now privately owned.

THE VILLAGE AND HOTEL, GARTOCHARN

A 5755

Like Croftamie, Gartocharn largely consists of a mixture of houses lining both sides of the old military road from Dumbarton to Stirling. The village is overlooked by Duncryne Hill, the summit of which affords excellent views of Loch Lomond. Many of the properties in this 1937 photograph still remain, although the Gartocharn Hotel is now The Hungry Monk and the post office opposite is now a private residence.

GARTOCHARN HOTEL.   5754.

Built in the 1800s, the Gartocharn Hotel was run by the McFarlan family for almost 100 years. One owner in the 1890s was a woman known as 'Old Lucky'. It appears to have been common practice in years gone by to prefix the word 'lucky' to a landlord or lady's surname because of the perception that they were always successful in business. On this occasion the landlady's name was dispensed with and the word 'old' used instead! In 1907 ownership transferred to the Dumbarton County Public House Trust, where it remained until the 1950s. The building still stands, although it has been extended several times, and is presently owned by the Cawley Group.

Gartocharn's Main Street has changed little since this picture was taken in 1953. The cottage on the extreme right is Clifton, built in 1851, and further along at the end of the row is the Gartocharn Hotel. There is still a garage, although it is now run by UK Petroleum. The shop adjacent to the garage is now Lomondview Stores and combines a general store and post office. In the 1800s, well before the advent of the post van, all of Gartocharn's mail was distributed from Alexandria Post Office and the postman had to walk from there to deliver it. The old public telephone kiosk beside the shop – referred to in the *Third Statistical Account* (1959) as an 'inestimable boon . . . taken advantage of widely' – has since been removed. In this age of mobile phones and e-mail perhaps that is not surprising, although even we can probably still identify with the comment made in the *Account* that occasionally 'there is some difficulty in getting connections made'!

When the Blane Valley railway line was originally proposed, it was intended that it would follow the valley before swinging north towards Aberfoyle and the Trossachs. However, the railway company ran into financial difficulties and as a result the line was terminated just past Blanefield, at Dumgoyne. Since there was already a station at Blanefield, and the original intention was that the next station on this line would be sited at Killearn, it was decided the station at Dumgoyne would be called Killearn! If this wasn't confusing enough, in 1882 the newly-formed Strathendrick & Aberfoyle Railway Company extended their line to take in Killearn proper and, for obvious reasons, named their new station Killearn as well! The station at Dumgoyne then became known as Old Killearn and was finally renamed Dumgoyne Station in 1896. The station was demolished after the line closed in 1959.

Beech Tree Cottage – now the Beech Tree Inn – stands on the A81, approximately 100 yards from where Dumgoyne Station stood. In fact the cottage was at one time occupied by the station's signalman. In this 1905 view the cottage was still a private dwelling although by the 1920s it had been converted into a grocer's shop, run successively by a Miss Linn and a Mrs Neilson. Later still, it was an antiques shop and in 1976 was converted for use as a restaurant. The original building has largely been retained, although a conservatory has now been added to the eastern gable.

DUMGOYNE.

Carrick's Tea Rooms, pictured in 1915, was beside a row of cottages situated on the Glasgow to Drymen road, near Dumgoyne Station. Although it was well-sited to catch passing trade from both road and rail travellers, it went out of business after the closure of the railway line in 1959. The cottage to the left of the picture served as the local post office for over a hundred years. However, a new post office was built nearby in the 1980s and nowadays the cottage is a private dwelling with its wall-mounted post box plastered over. All the cottages in the photograph still remain, although dormers have been added and the pitched roofs over the front entrances have been removed. Beyond the cottages is the railway level crossing, with Dumgoyne Hill dominating the background.

THE MOSS HOUSE, DUMGOYNE.

The Birthplace of George Buchanan, the Historian.

Situated in the grounds of the former estate of Mid-Leowen, Moss House dates from the eighteenth century and stands on the site of earlier houses owned by the Buchanan family. One of these was the birthplace of George Buchanan who was born in the early 1500s (there is some dubiety whether it was 1506 or 1507). Buchanan is reputed to have been schooled at nearby Killearn and went on to become one of Scotland's most eminent scholars, eventually tutoring the young King James VI. In the late 1700s Moss House was owned by James Finlay, a well-known Glasgow merchant, who is said to have entertained Richard Arkwright (inventor of the Spinning Jenny) there. In 1906 an extension designed by the famous architect, Charles Rennie McIntosh, was added to the property. However, this extension was demolished in 1969 so that today Moss House largely retains the appearance of this earlier photograph.

The Halfway House – now the Carbeth Inn – on the old Glasgow to Drymen turnpike road apparently took its name from the fact that it lay equidistant between these two communities. Said to be over two hundred years old, the inn is referred to by Sir Walter Scott in *Rob Roy*, published in 1817. In the novel Baillie Nicol Jarvie stays at the Halfway House, describing it afterwards as a 'most miserable alehouse'. However, this does not seem to have been a commonly-held point of view and, over the years, it has been a popular stopping point for many, including climbers visiting the Whangie (a narrow ravine on nearby Auchineden Hill) and residents from the nearby Carbeth Huts (visible on the hill beyond the inn). The entrance way of the building has been altered and a very small extension added where the 'Sitting Rooms' sign is. The old-fashioned petrol pumps have now gone and the wall on the left has been extended to make an enclosed outside eating area.

TWO ACRES. STOCKIEMUIR ROAD.

After the First World War a Holiday Fellowship Camp was established on Carbeth Estate by three ex-servicemen, mainly to provide inexpensive holiday accommodation in the countryside. An area known as Two Acres, alongside the Stockiemuir Road, was acquired and initially tents were erected there. By the 1930s residential huts had been built by unemployed Clydesiders and in the early 1940s more were erected by families (mostly from Clydebank) made homeless by enemy air attacks. In summers gone by the area would be bursting at the seams with families eager to enjoy the fresh country air. The early residents in this picture were certainly self-sufficient, having, amongst other things, their own – albeit small – shop!

Although they were built on ground leased from the estate, the huts themselves belonged to the tenants and were built using whatever material was available. Over the years they have been improved upon, but for many years there were no drainage facilities and there are still no mains supplies of gas, electricity or running water. However, there was certainly no lack of recreational facilities! The number of huts now stands at over 200, some of which are still owned by the same family, having been handed down from generation to generation.

Carbeth Swimming Pond.

The Swimming Pond was an extremely popular haunt of the Carbeth 'hutters'. The area was well-organised with the pond being fenced off in parts and life belts provided. There were also diving boards for the braver swimmers.

Blanefield had its own railway station and by the early 1900s it had been taken over by the North British Railway Company. No doubt in common with other rural stations, it was at that time in need of upgrading and it was said to have lacked a water supply and proper sanitation. This was alleged to be due to the North British blocking a proposal to have the station and stationmaster's house included in the newly-formed local water board district. Another complaint appears to have been the lack of a cattle pen, despite the fact that local farmers used the railway for transporting cattle. Beyond the station can be seen the housing on Station Road. To the right of this is Anthony Coubrough's Blanefield Calico Print Works, and one of its two chimneys. The taller of the two – the 160 foot high Great Chimney Stack – was demolished in February 1910.

This property, built by two brothers, is situated on the main road through Blanefield and was a grocer's shop before later becoming Blanefield Post Office. The building – still the post office – is largely unchanged from this view, although the chimneys have gone and the outbuilding has been replaced by a garage.

THE SCHOOL, BLANEFIELD

At a meeting of local property owners in 1780 it was resolved to build a parish school at Netherton. A year later, on land gifted by a local landowner, James Craig of Ballewen, a school and schoolhouse were erected at Thorn of Cuilt. Some years later it was decided that the 7 feet floor to ceiling height of the rooms was insufficient and in 1802 work was carried out to increase this by 6 feet – achieved by lowering the floor of the school! Over time the school became inadequate and it was subsequently demolished. A replacement (pictured) was built on the same site in 1834 and was extended in 1875. It continued to serve children from Blanefield and the surrounding area until 1966, when a new primary school was opened in Kirkburn Road, Strathblane. Ironically, when the first Netherton village school was built, children from Strathblane had to travel to Netherton for schooling; nowadays children from Netherton have to travel to Strathblane!

Station Road, Blanefield. On the left-hand side of the picture are the properties on Burnside Row which were known locally as 'The Palace'. At one time these were occupied by workers from the nearby Blanefield Calico Print Works which opened in 1841 and closed in 1898. The property set further back on the hill is the former stationmaster's house (now Bluebell Cottage) and alongside it is the station. Nowadays, modern housing has replaced the Row and the station buildings (apart from the Stationmaster's house) have been demolished.

Strathblane's war memorial was unveiled on 21 August 1921 by the Duke of Montrose. It is made from Doddington stone and the cost of £800 was paid by public subscription. Its designer, Sir Robert Lorimer, was also partly responsible for the design of the Scottish War Memorial at Edinburgh Castle. Although it has always been sited at the corner of Glasgow Road and Campsie Dene Road, it was moved approximately 50 yards to improve this junction. The shop to left of picture is still standing, although it is now occupied by Netherton Antiques.

Glasgow Road, Blanefield, *c.* 1900. Beyond Woodbank Cottage on the right is a tenement building which was erected in 1895. This contained private accommodation, a shop and, when this photograph was taken, Danny McGregor's restaurant and hall. The latter was apparently extremely large, running the full length of the basement and a diverse range of activities were held in it, including picnics and carpet bowls! Opposite it is the Netherton Inn which was built in the 1850s and is now called the Blane Valley Inn.

By the turn of the last century large villas had been built on either side of Glasgow Road. Further along from the villas, half-hidden by the trees and situated near the site of the old St Kessog's Well, is Netherton House. Although it is now a private residence, the house has had many uses over the years: a Rechabite Hall (the Order of Rechabites was a society devoted to abstention from alcohol), a police station and a doctor's surgery. Just out of view, to the left, is the Village Hall, known as Edmonstone Hall. This was gifted to the village by the Edmonstone family of Duntreath and was opened in October 1926. The road on the left, Craigmarloch View, now leads to a modern housing estate.

NETHERTON, STRATHBLANE.

Netherton – or Caravan – Park complete with goalposts. A printworks was formerly sited here. Although these have long since gone, the houses built to accommodate the print workers remain – the one exception being Sunnyside, which was hit in 1941 by a stray bomb. Known as the 'new hooses', they are on the left of the picture. In front of the houses, and marked by the stone walls, is the line of the underground pipe which takes Glasgow's water supply from Loch Katrine.

Strathblane Village Club, pictured shortly after its opening in 1911, was built to commemorate the coronation of King George V. The funds were provided by A.F. Yarrow, a successful Glasgow shipbuilder who stayed at Campsie Dene, near the war memorial. The club had accommodation for a caretaker, a reading room, a billiards room (which could also be used as a meeting room), and a library. Membership was confined to residents of Strathblane aged sixteen years and over. Nowadays, it is used by the community for whist drives, dances, etc.

The Home Hospital, Strathblane.

R. McNeil
Post Office,
Strathblane.

The Children's Home Hospital was originally based in rented accommodation in Aberfoyle. When new premises were sought, opposition was encountered from Aberfoyle residents, and the hospital was built on Shillin Hill to the south of Strathblane. Officially opened on 20 June 1913, the hospital was intended as a convalescent home and only accepted children from Glasgow up to the age of twelve years who suffered from tuberculosis of the bones and joints (not lungs). For a short time, however, children suffering from acute rheumatism were admitted (in fact, an extension was built to house these patients) and eventually it accepted children with incipient TB. The children were given lessons and could receive visitors, although this was discouraged – in 1905 visitors could come only every three months, unless for special reasons! By 1942, however, the rules were more relaxed as visiting was permitted twice a week. The hospital was taken over by the Health Board in 1948 for the care of physically and mentally handicapped children. It closed in 1994 and its site is now occupied by housing.

The seventeenth century Kirkhouse Inn stands at the junction of two major roads which ran from Glasgow to Drymen and Lennoxtown to Drymen. Originally it was a toll house and was also a staging post for coaches. Nowadays, with the expansion of Strathblane, it stands at the eastern boundary of the village.